#SOCIALWOR[KERLIFE]

A SNARKY ADULT COLORING BOOK FOR SOCIAL WORKERS

M000159440

DEATH BEFORE DECAF

SSION NOTES

Want free goodies?
Email us at freebies@pbleu.com

@papeteriebleu

Papeterie Bleu

Shop our other books at
www.pbleu.com

Wholesale distribution through Ingram Content Group
www.ingramcontent.com/publishers/distribution/wholesale

For questions and customer service, email us at
support@pbleu.com

HERE'S TO ANOTHER DAY OF OUTWARD SMILES AND INWARD SCREAMS.

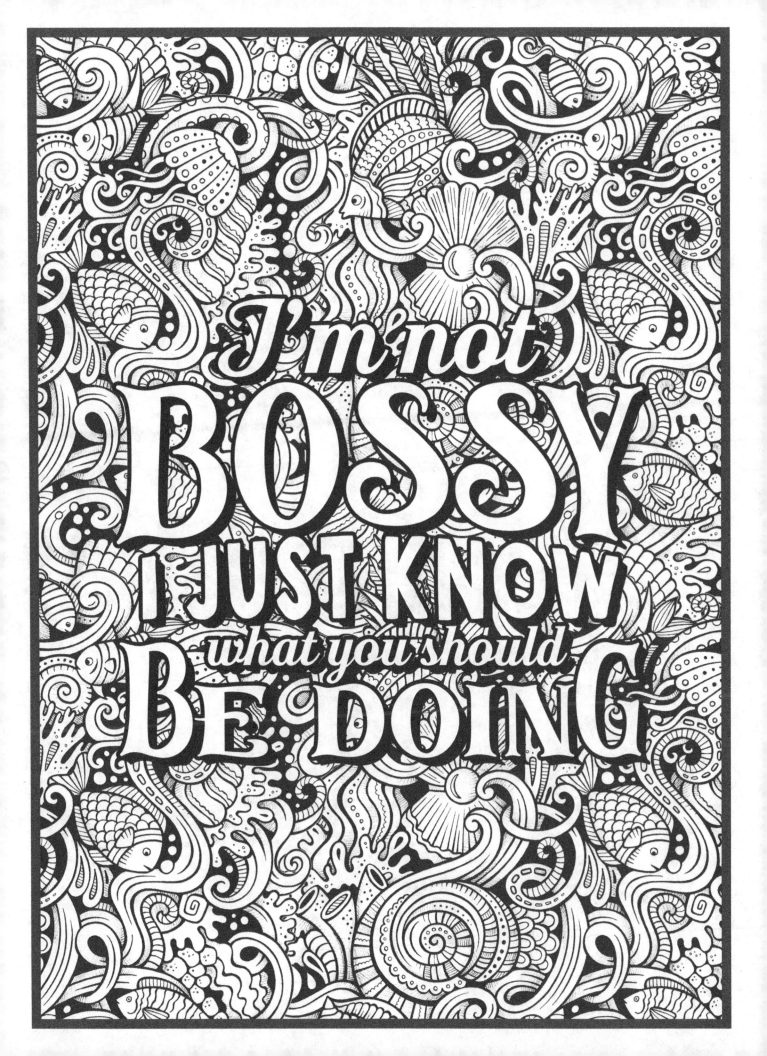

I'm not BOSSY I JUST KNOW what you should BE DOING

I AM A SOCIAL WORKER: TO SAVE TIME, LET'S JUST ASSUME I AM ALWAYS Right!

I'VE SEEN MONKEY FECES FIGHTS AT THE ZOO MORE Organized THAN MY WORKPLACE!

"I DO THIS FOR THE MONEY!" SAID NO SOCIAL WORKER EVER!

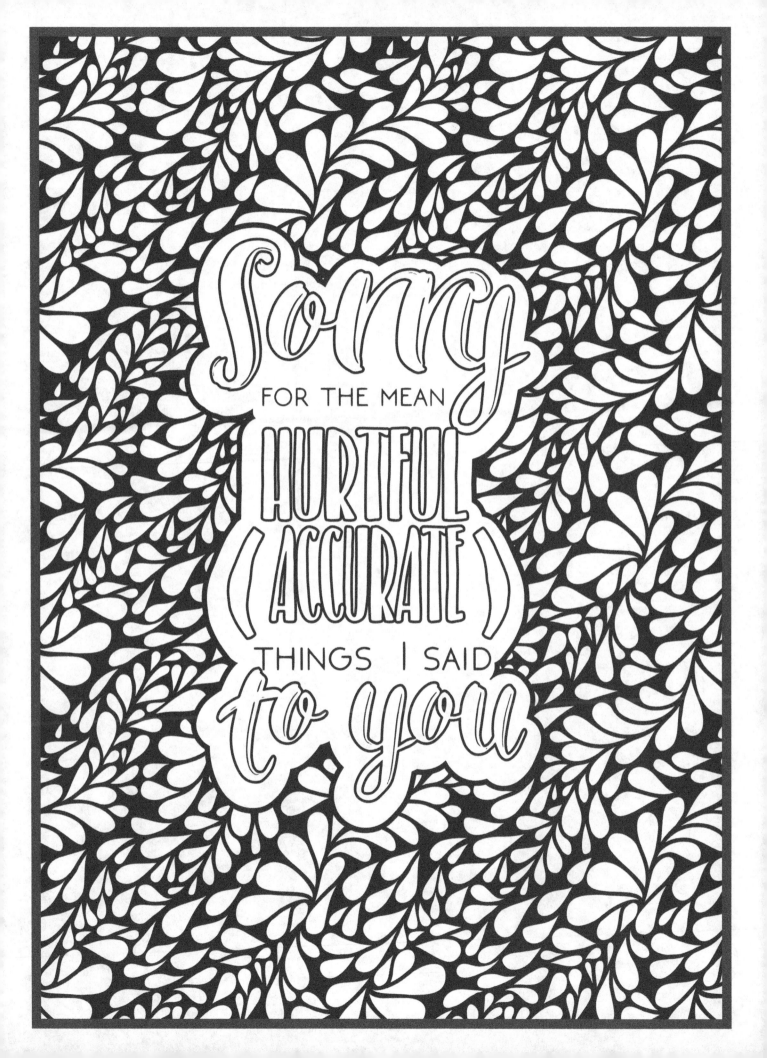

Sorry FOR THE MEAN HURTFUL (ACCURATE) THINGS I SAID to you

THANK YOU *student loans* FOR HELPING ME GET THROUGH SCHOOL I DON'T THINK I CAN EVER *Repay You*

HOW MANY SOCIAL WORKERS DOES IT TAKE TO CHANGE A lightbulb? ONE. BUT THE LIGHTBULB HAS TO WANT TO CHANGE

SOCIAL WORK: YOU'RE NOT IN IT FOR THE income YOU'RE IN IT FOR THE OUTCOME

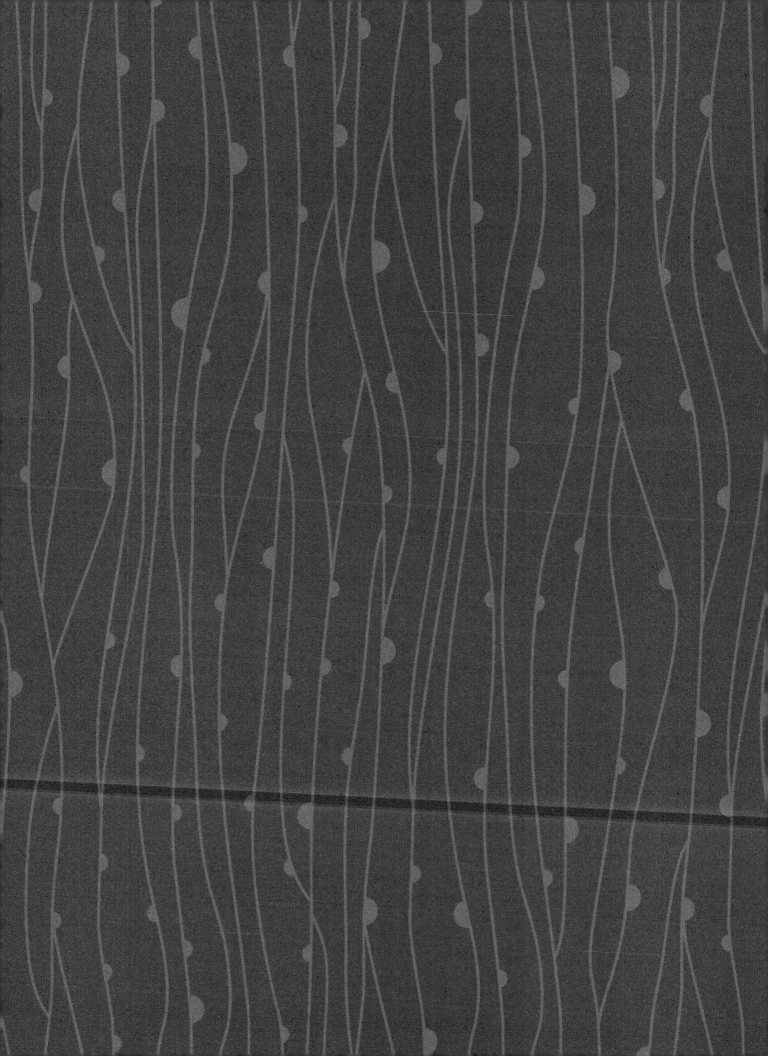

SOCIAL WORKER.
LIKE A SUPER HERO. ONLY REAL

SUPER SOCIAL WORKER

THE Hardest PART OF MY Job IS BEING NICE TO People

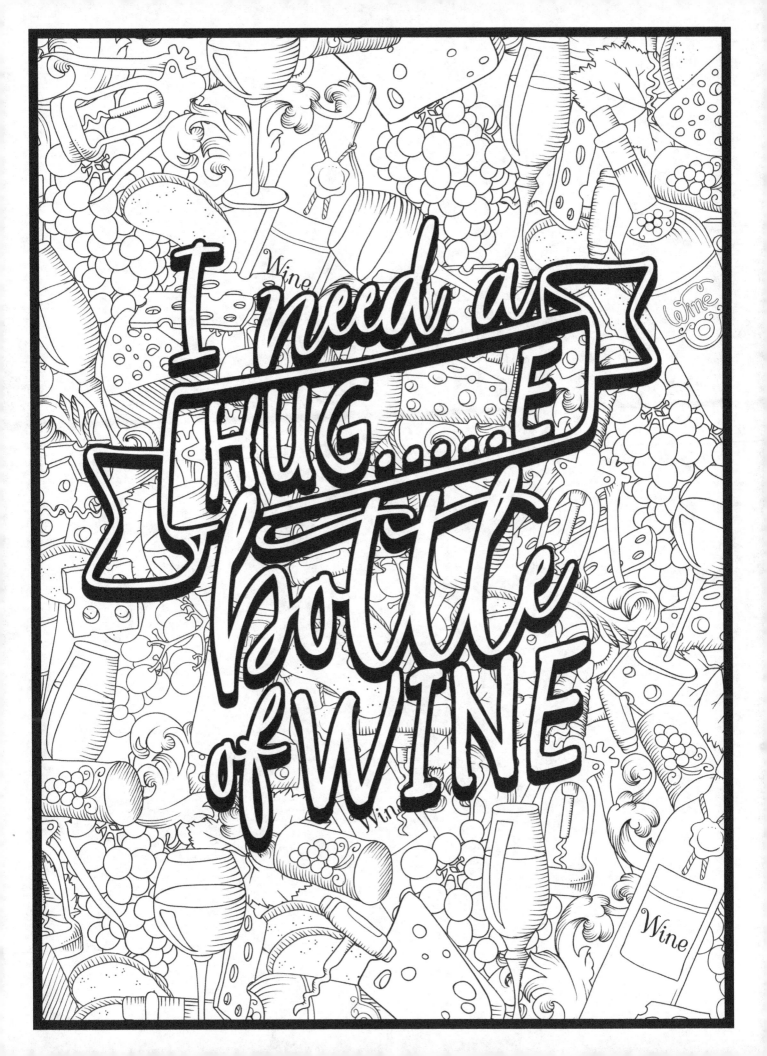

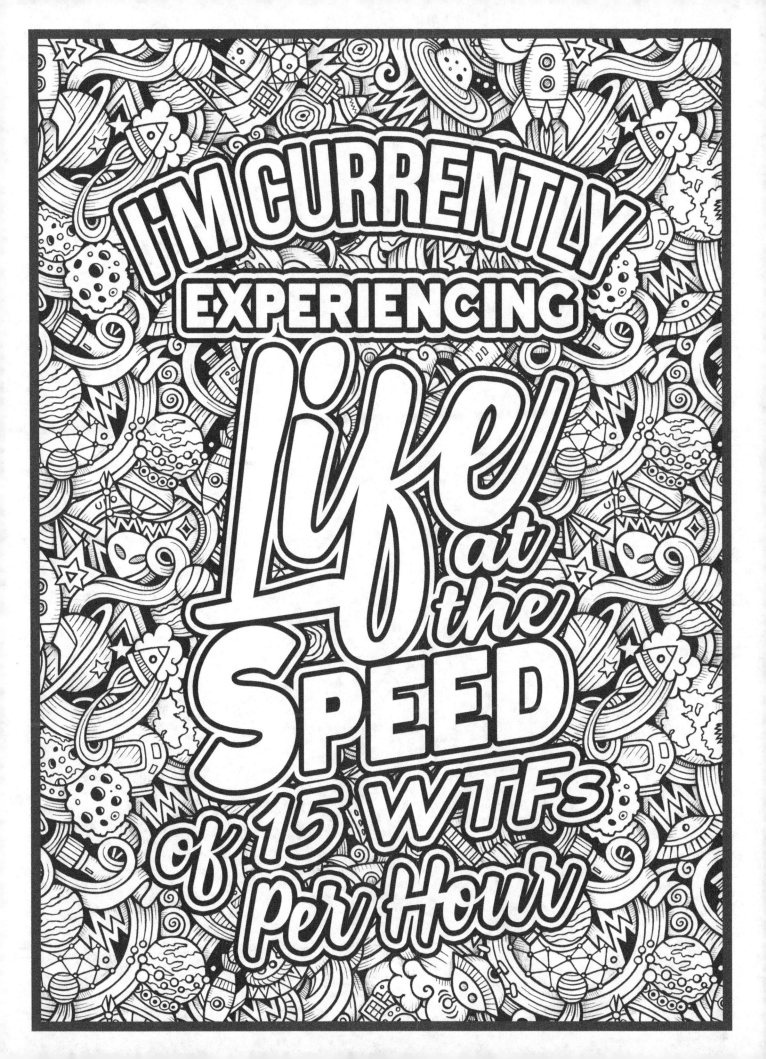

I'M CURRENTLY EXPERIENCING Life at the SPEED of 15 WTFs Per Hour

SOME PEOPLE NEED a high five. In the FACE. WITH A CHAIR.

BEING A SOCIAL WORKER IS EASY. IT'S LIKE RIDING A BIKE. EXCEPT THE BIKE IS ON FIRE. YOU'RE ON FIRE. EVERYTHING IS ON FIRE.

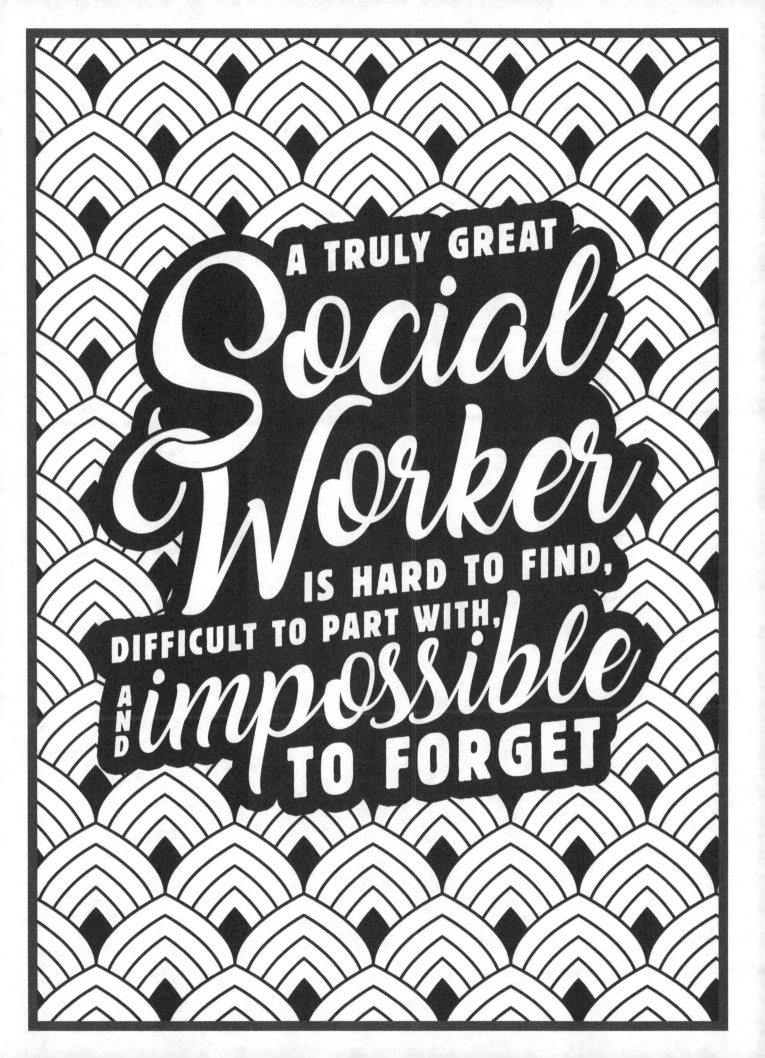

A TRULY GREAT Social Worker IS HARD TO FIND, DIFFICULT TO PART WITH, AND impossible TO FORGET

WHEN I GET OFF THE PHONE WITH YOU, I'M GOING TO TELL MY CO-WORKERS HOW STUPID YOU ARE.

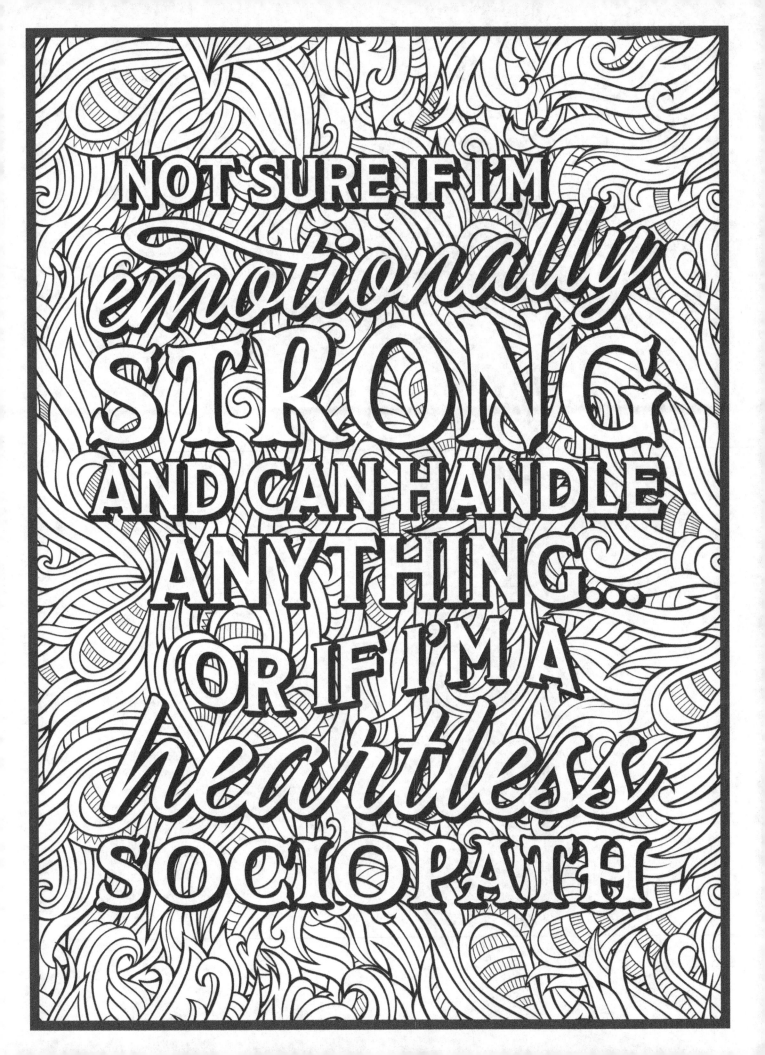

⚠ WARNING ⚠

TO AVOID SERIOUS INJURY

DON'T TELL ME HOW TO DO MY JOB

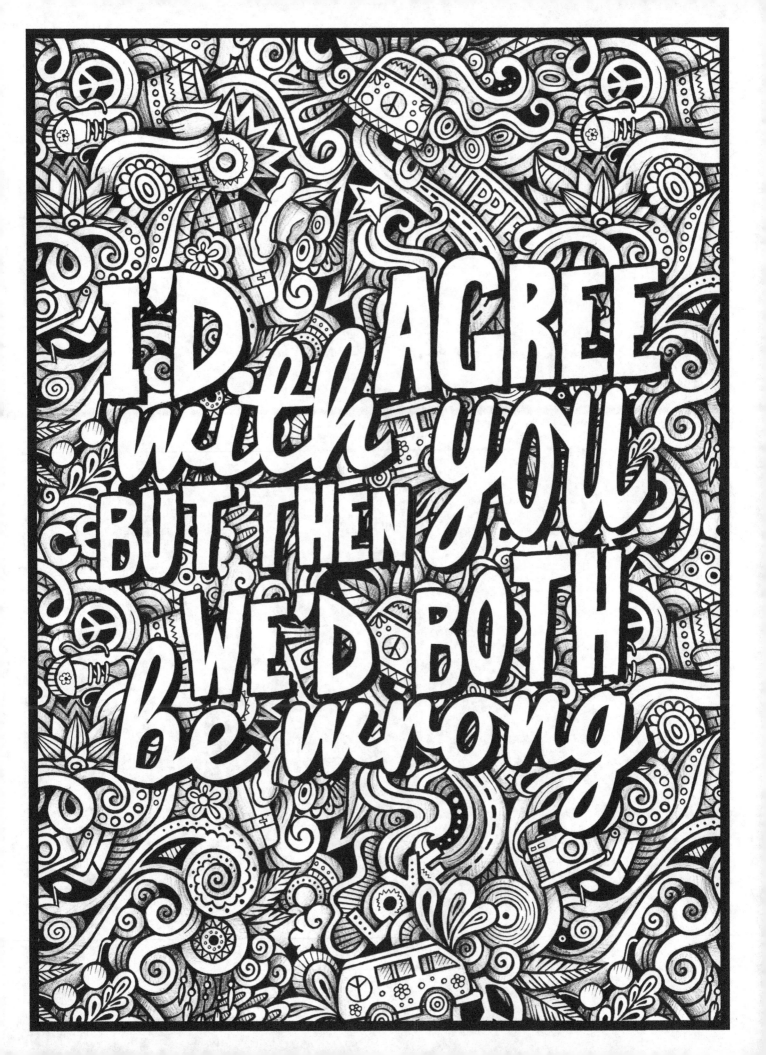

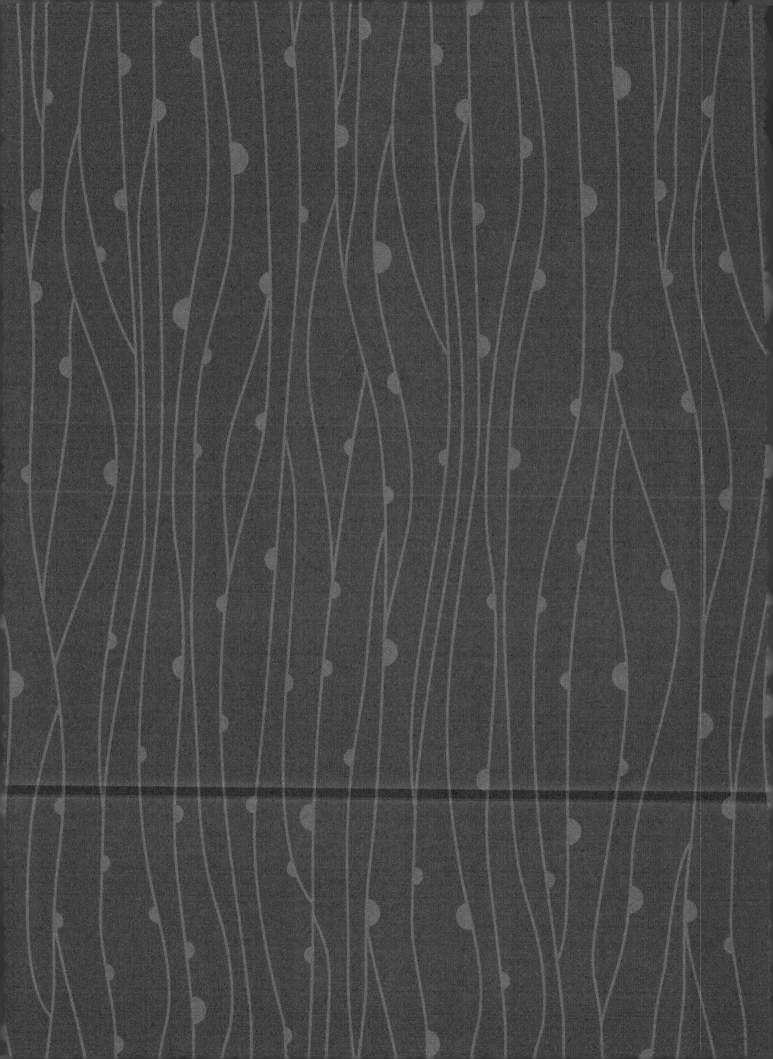

The moment that you REALIZE that you've been at work for only an HOUR.

My lack OF INNER PEACE IS STRESSING me out

I'M TOO HUNGRY to sleep, BUT I'M TOO TIRED TO FIND SOMETHING to eat

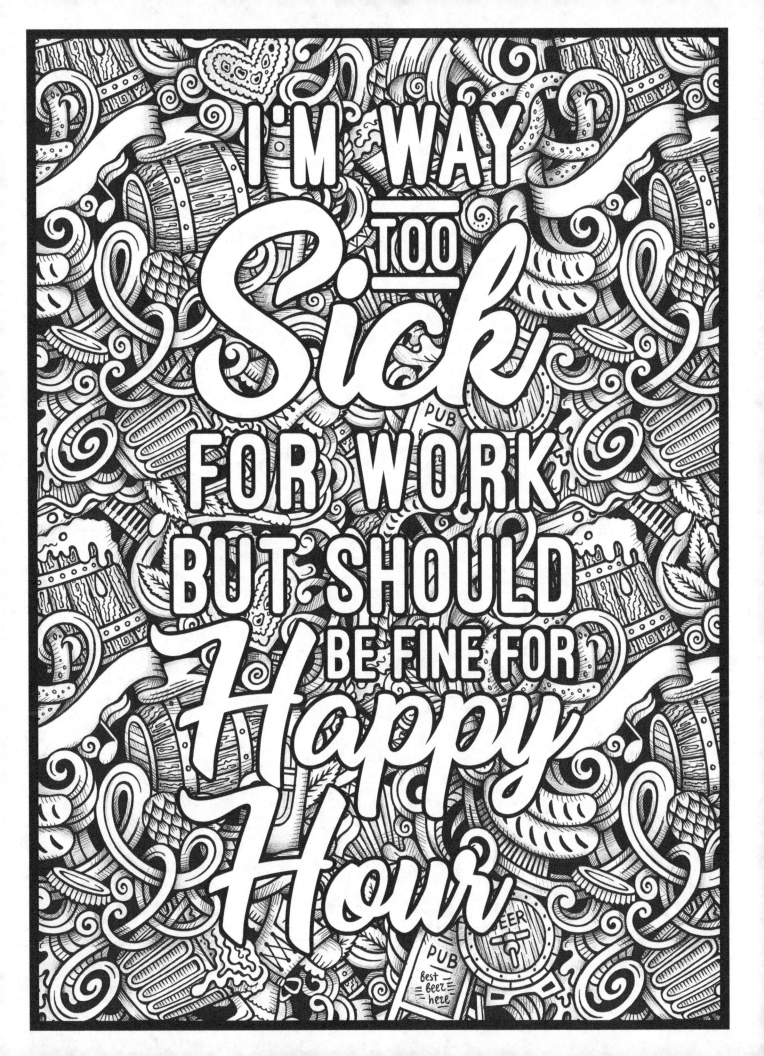

I'M WAY TOO Sick FOR WORK BUT SHOULD BE FINE FOR Happy Hour

My opinion OFFENDED YOU? YOU SHOULD HEAR the ones I KEEP TO MYSELF.

I already WANT to TAKE A NAP TOMORROW

Me? Crazy? I should get down off this unicorn and slap you!

Better days are coming. They are called "Saturday" and "Sunday"

Let's burn that bridge when we get there.

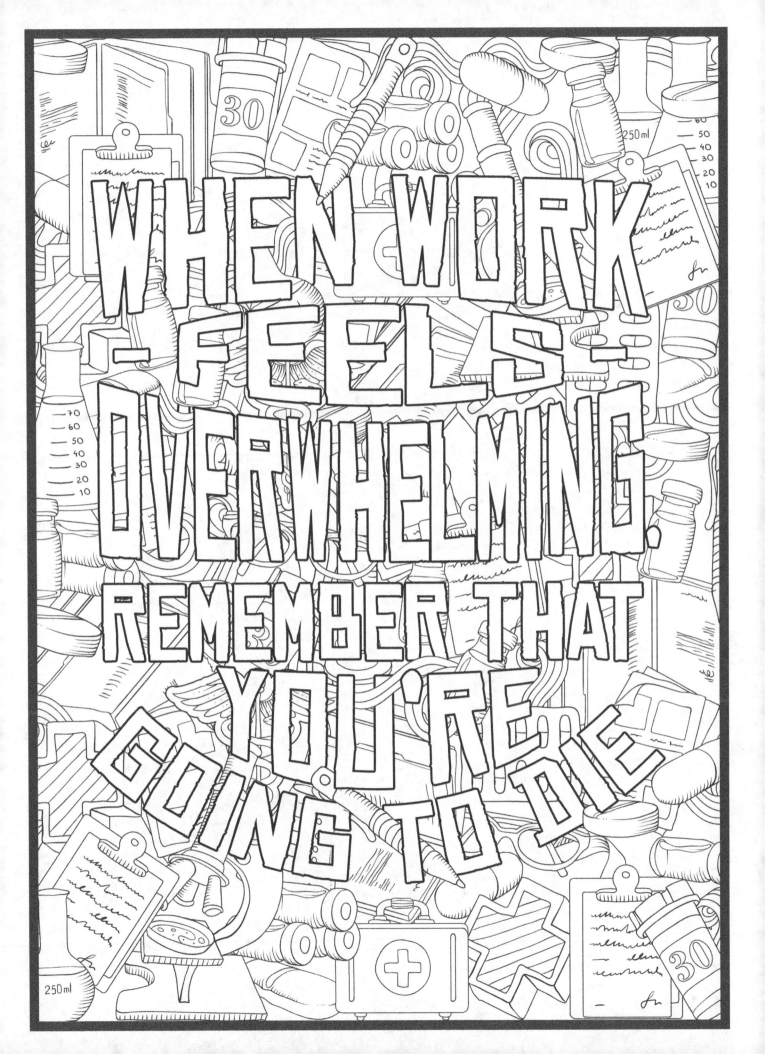

WHEN WORK FEELS OVERWHELMING. REMEMBER THAT YOU'RE GOING TO DIE

Happiness is not Having to set an alarm for TOMORROW

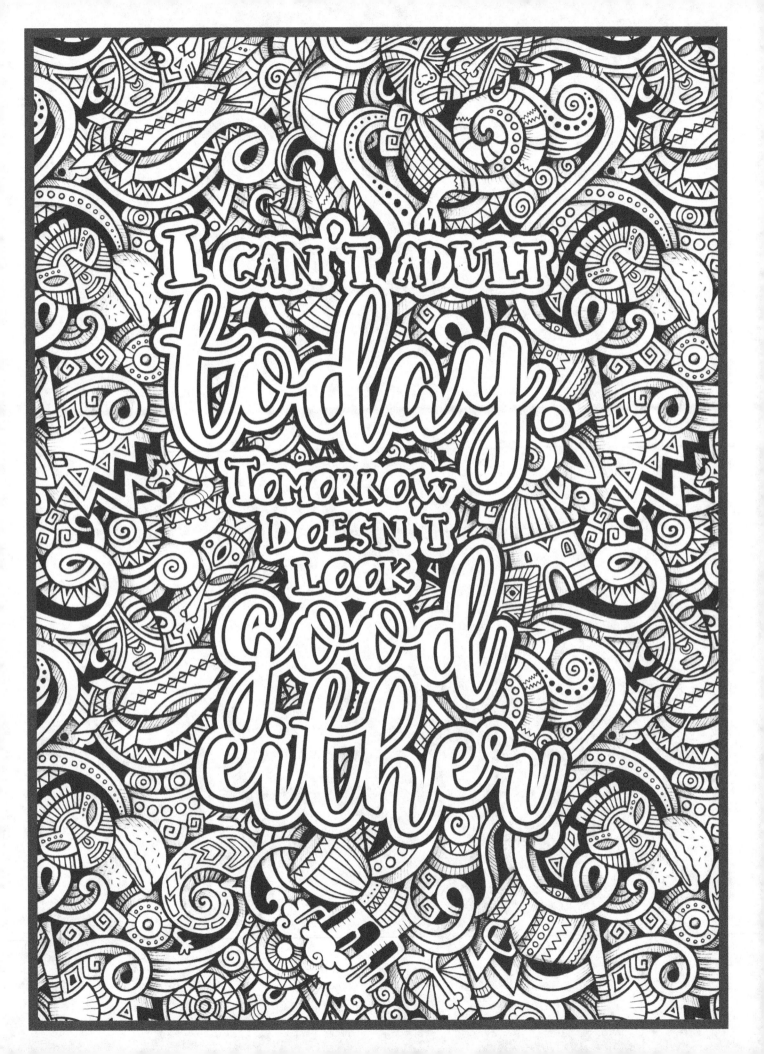

I can't adult today. Tomorrow doesn't look good either

I'm allergic TO STUPIDITY. I BREAK OUT in sarcasm

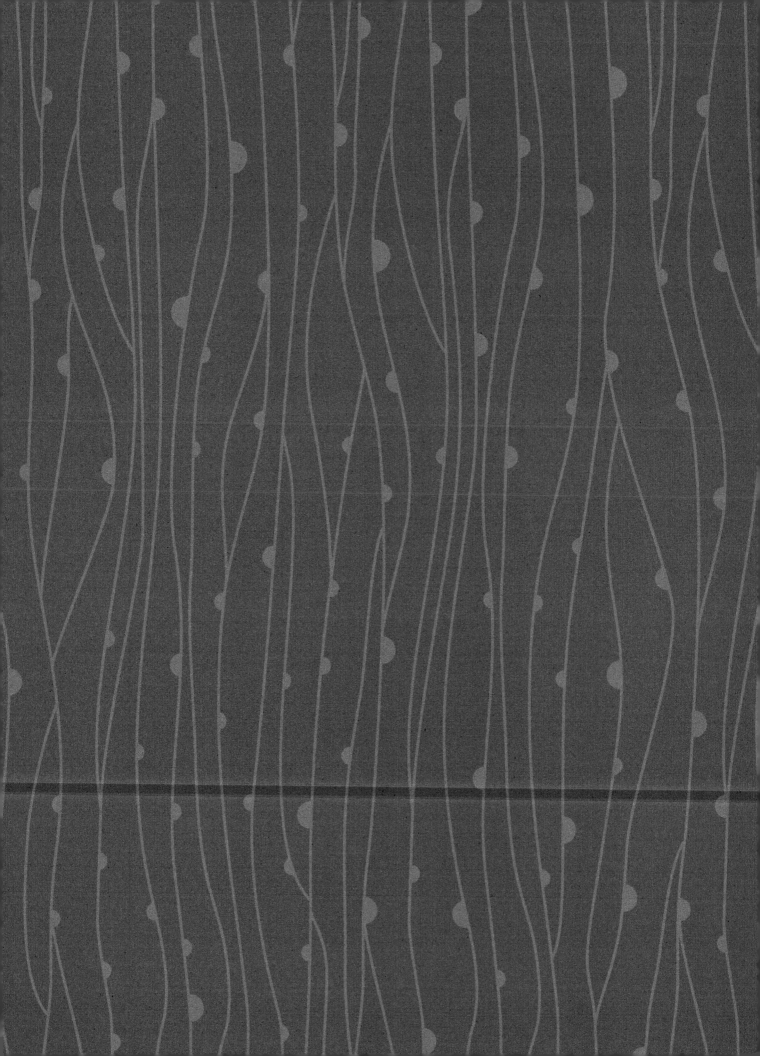

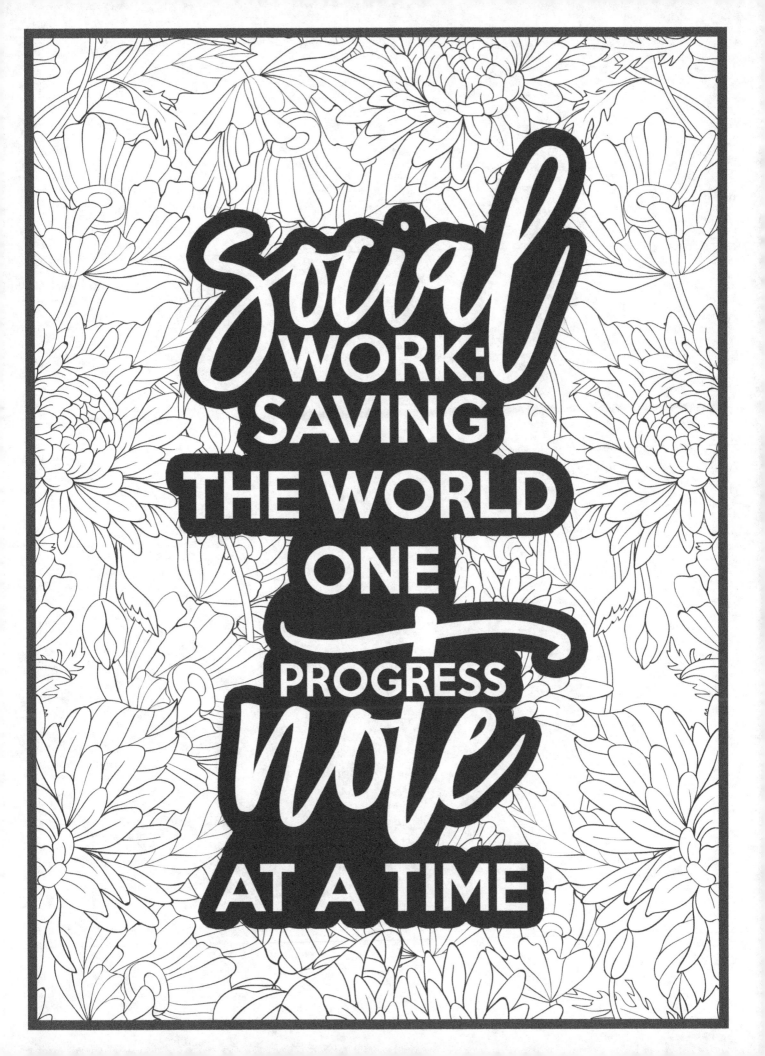

Social WORK: SAVING THE WORLD ONE PROGRESS note AT A TIME

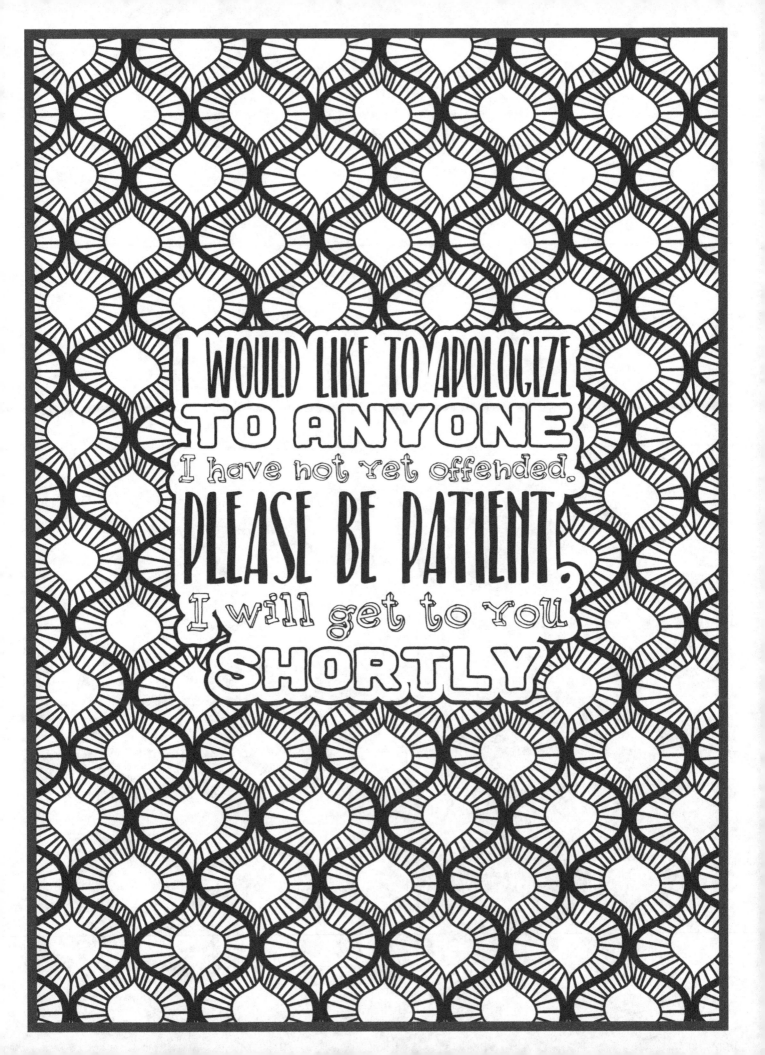

I WOULD LIKE TO APOLOGIZE TO ANYONE I have not yet offended. PLEASE BE PATIENT, I will get to you SHORTLY

MY DEGREE IN SOCIAL WORK MAKES ME HIGHLY QUALIFIED TO JUDGE EVERYONE

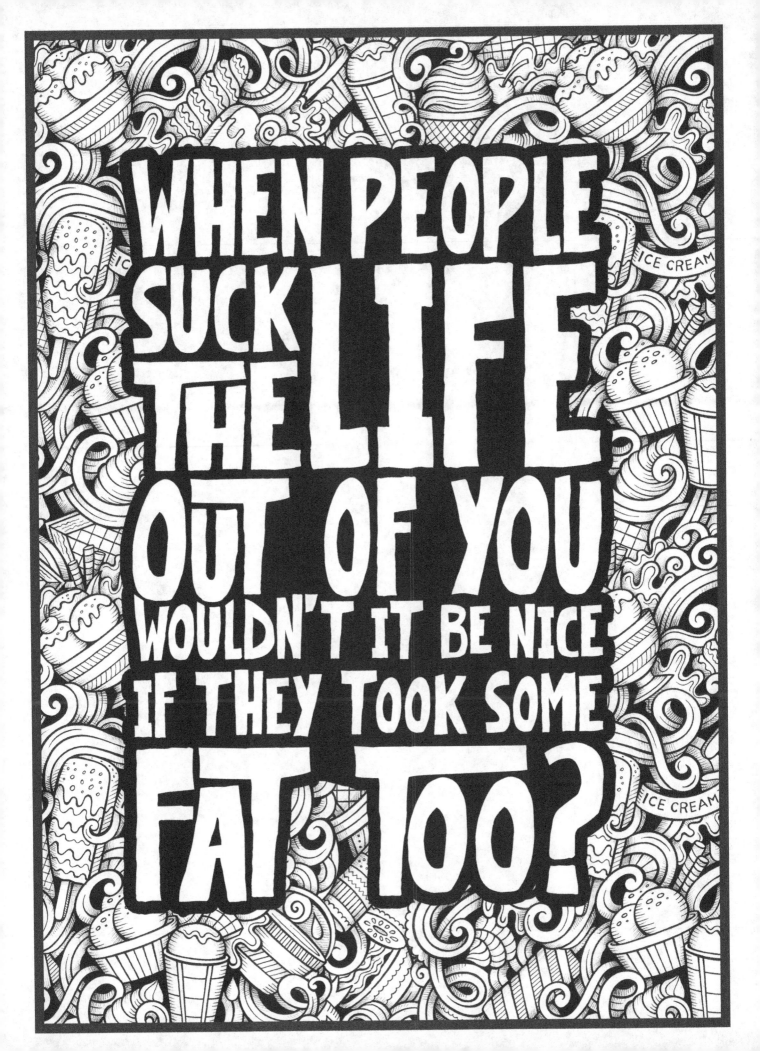

WHEN PEOPLE SUCK THE LIFE OUT OF YOU WOULDN'T IT BE NICE IF THEY TOOK SOME FAT TOO?

If there was a problem Yo, I'll solve it #SocialWorkerLife

DOCUMENTING IS MY cardio

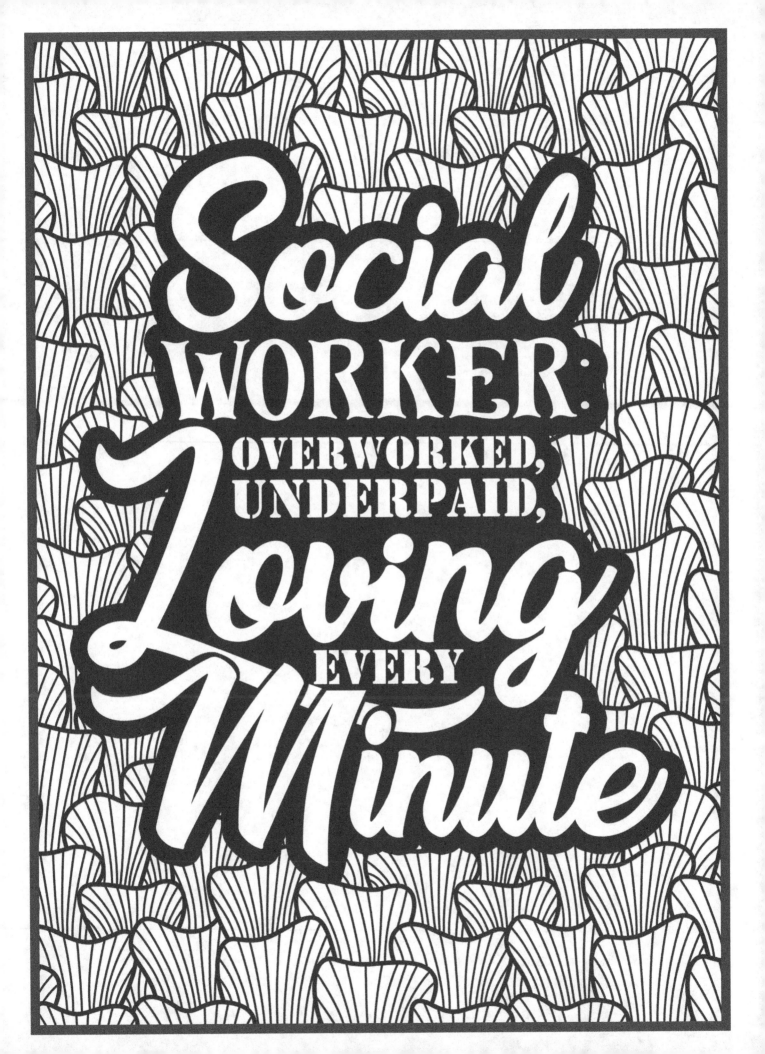

Social WORKER: OVERWORKED, UNDERPAID, Loving EVERY Minute

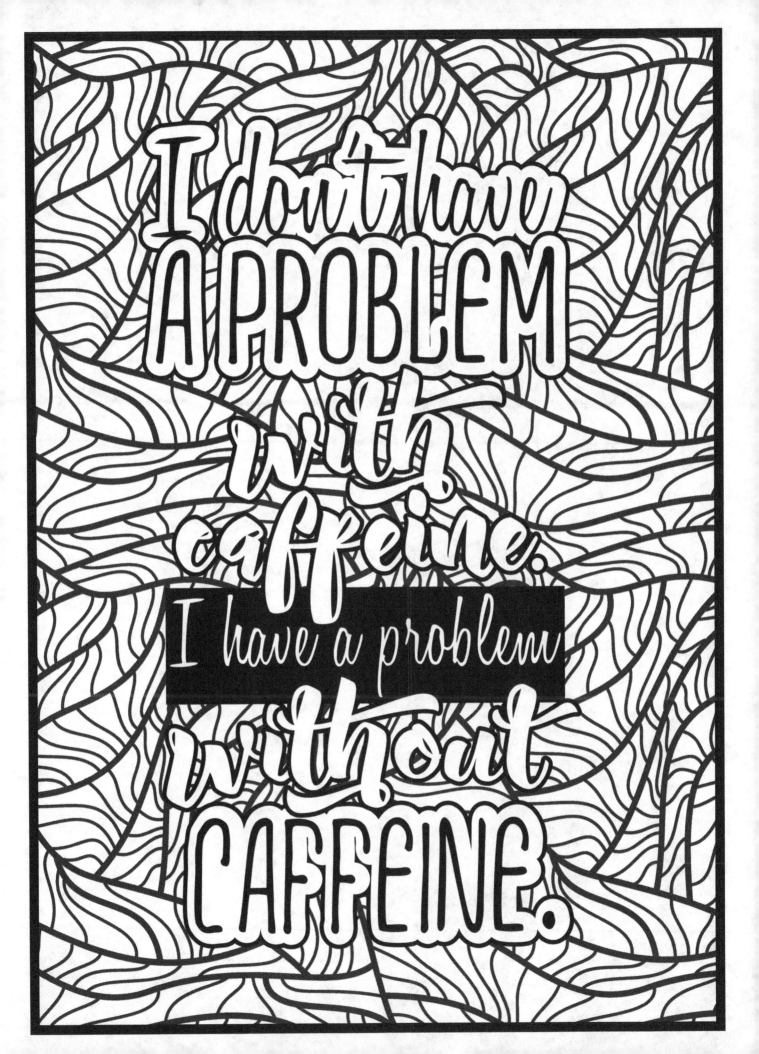

I don't have A PROBLEM with caffeine. I have a problem without CAFFEINE.

Ugh. I can't Even

I AM NOT SOMEONE YOU CAN PUT ON SPEAKERPHONE

The BAGS under my eyes ARE PRADA

FREE PDF DOWNLOAD OF THIS BOOK

www.pbleu.com/socialwork

YOUR DOWNLOAD CODE: SW3773

 @papeteriebleu

 Papeterie Bleu

Want free goodies?
Email us at freebies@pbleu.com

@papeteriebleu

Papeterie Bleu

Shop our other books at
www.pbleu.com

Wholesale distribution through Ingram Content Group
www.ingramcontent.com/publishers/distribution/wholesale

For questions and customer service, email us at
support@pbleu.com